Grandma

I Want to Hear About Your

Life

Published by Midsummer Bloom Books

First Edition: March 2025
Printed in the United States of America

Contents

Your Stories Are Family Treasures

You know what's amazing about your kitchen, Grandma? It's not just those cookies you bake or that soup nobody can quite figure out. It's how you always have a story ready while you're cooking - like when you dig out that old recipe card and start telling us about where it came from. The way your face lights up when you say "Oh, that reminds me..." - we know we're in for something good.

This book is all yours, Grandma. A place to jot down memories about that little girl who ended up becoming our grandmother. Remember those summer days when you were a kid? The games you played? Those silly things that kept you up at night dreaming? The stuff that made you laugh so hard you couldn't breathe?

You've seen it all, haven't you? From playing hopscotch to raising kids of your own, from that first paycheck to the day you became "Grandma." Each bit of your life has helped write our family's story.

Bet there are some stories you haven't told us yet - maybe about times when you had to be brave, or those love notes you and Grandpa wrote, or how you figured things out when they got tough. And those family traditions we all love? You're probably the only one who knows how they really started.

Take your time with these pages. Tell us about the songs that were popular back then, stuff you learned the hard way, and those moments that still make you grin. Tell us what your world was like and how you helped shape the one we live in now.

Because here's the thing, Grandma - your stories aren't just old memories. They're like pieces of you we get to keep forever. And we can't wait to hear them all.

How to Use This Book

Throughout this book, you'll find thought-starters and memory prompts beneath each question. These are simply suggestions to spark ideas and memories - feel free to use them as inspiration or take your story in completely different directions. There are no right or wrong ways to share your life stories here. Just enjoy looking back on the path that led you here.

Dearest Grandma, with your special smile,

Your love has touched us all this while,

Through years of hugs and laughter sweet,

Your story makes our hearts complete.

Tell us your journey - every precious page.

1

Days of Long Ago

Like treasured pearls on a golden thread, our family stories shine through generations. Each precious tale of those who came before us warms our hearts and lights our way.

Ancestral Roots

Tell us about the lands our family came from. What stories have been passed down about our ancestors' journey and the lives they built in their new home?

What places did our ancestors first call home?

• Original homeland

• Family village

What language or dialect did they speak?

• Family language

• Local words

When did our family first settle here?

• First move date

• Arrival place

Family Tree Tales

Each branch of our family tree holds memories of those who shaped our legacy, their lives echoing through generations in ways both seen and unseen.

Think back to the characters who colored your early years. Which personalities stand out in your memory?

Tell us about a favorite aunt or uncle who brought something special to your childhood.

• Best aunt/uncle

• Fun memories

What made your grandparents' house special?

• Their house

• Visit times

Which uncle or aunt influenced you most?

• Close relative

• Wise teaching

The Old Family Home

Behind those familiar doors lay a world of memories. Every corner held stories, every room echoed with laughter and life.

Describe the house where you spent your childhood. What details do you remember most vividly – the sounds, the smells, the special corners that held your dreams?

Which scenes from your childhood home still feel alive today? Paint us a picture of:

• Front door

• Family room

What did your childhood bedroom look like?

• Bed space

• Room style

Which room held most family gatherings?

• Main room

• Together place

Mother's Ways

My mother moved through life with grace and wisdom, showing me what strength looked like in daily moments.

What was special about your mother's approach to life? Share the lessons she taught, the habits she kept, and the love she showed in her own unique way.

What daily routine did your mother never skip?

• Daily task

• Always done

What special dish was she known for?

• Best dish

• Famous food

What saying did she often repeat?

• Often said

• Life wisdom

Father's Presence

My father carried quiet wisdom in his steps. His presence filled our home with security and guidance, his principles shaping our family's foundation.

Tell us about your father's role in shaping your world. What moments with him left lasting impressions on your heart and mind?

What work did your father do?

- Main job

- Work life

What skill did your father teach you?

- Key skill

- Life lesson

How did he spend his free time?

- Daily hobbies

- Weekend activities

Kitchen Memories

Our kitchen danced with aromas of fresh bread, simmering soups, and love stirred into every meal. It was where family stories unfolded over mixing bowls and warm ovens.

What scenes played out in your childhood kitchen? Remember the aromas, the recipes, and the gathering of family around the table.

What was your favorite breakfast growing up?

- Morning meal

- Special treats

Which holiday dish meant celebration time?

- Festival food

- Special cooking

What kitchen tool brings back memories?

- Kitchen things

- Cooking items

Family Traditions

*"Tradition is not to preserve the ashes but to pass on the flame." -
Gustav Mahler*

Which customs made your family unique? Share about the special
practices that brought meaning to everyday life and celebrations.
What holiday tradition never changed?

• Year custom

• Holiday must

What morning routine did everyone follow?

• Wake routine

• Start day

How did seasons change family activities?

• Seasonal tasks

• Weather customs

Holiday Times

Each holiday brought its own magic that we anticipated all year. These celebrations marked our seasons with joy, creating memories that would warm future generations.

How did your family make holidays special? Tell us about the traditions, decorations, and celebrations that marked these occasions.

What decoration always meant holiday time?

• Special ornaments

• Home decoration

Which holiday food did everyone wait for?

• Festival meals

• Family favorites

What gift-giving tradition did you have?

• Present customs

• Giving ways

Sibling Stories

"Siblings are the people we practice on, the people who teach us about fairness and cooperation and kindness and caring." - Pamela Dugdale

Share about growing up with your brothers and sisters. What adventures, conflicts, and tender moments shaped your relationships?

What was your favorite joint adventure?

• Play day

• Good times

Which sibling skill impressed you most?

• Special talent

• Brother/sister strength

How did you handle disagreements?

• Problem solving

• Peace making

Neighborhood Life

"A neighborhood is where the world begins." - *Frederick Buechner*

What was life like in your childhood neighborhood? Remember the friends, the daily rhythms, and the sense of community that surrounded you.

Who lived in the house next door?

• Close neighbors

• Regular visits

What games did neighborhood kids play?

• Street games

• Group activities

What local shop did you visit daily?

• Regular store

• Corner market

Family Treasures

Some treasures shine with gold, others glow with memories alone.
Each inherited item carries stories of those who held it before.

Which cherished items have been passed down through generations?
Share the stories behind these special keepsakes and their meaning.

What is the oldest item in your family?

• Ancient piece

• Special heirloom

What handmade item still remains?

• Crafted treasure

• Handwork piece

What kitchen item passed through generations?

• Cooking tools

• Special utensils

2

Growing Up in Your Time

Sweet memories of ribbon bows and Sunday dresses, of Mama's cookies cooling on windowsills. Your childhood was wrapped in love, simple joys, and tender care.

Daily Life Then

Life moved at a different rhythm in those days. Without screens and devices, our days filled with real adventures, imagination, and the simple pleasure.

How different was a child's day in your time? Tell us about the simple routines and activities that filled your early years.

What was your morning routine when you first woke up?

- First tasks

- Morning rules

What activities filled your typical morning hours?

- Play time

- Home help

Tell us about breakfast traditions in your childhood home.

- Food eat

- Table sit

Childhood Games

We made our own entertainment then – hopscotch drawn with chalk, marbles that were precious as gems, jump rope rhymes that echoed down the street.

What games brought joy to your childhood? Share about the ways children created fun before television and technology.

What outdoor games did you play in your neighborhood?

- Street games

- Yard play

How did you spend rainy day hours inside?

- Home games

- Room play

What games did you create using simple objects?

- Found toys

- New games

Early Friends

"A friend is one of the nicest things you can have and one of the best things you can be." – Winnie the Pooh

Who were your first playmates? Remember those early friendships and the adventures you shared in those innocent days.

Who was your very first childhood friend?

• First meeting

• Play memories

What games did your neighborhood friends create?

• Group fun

• Made games

Which friend's house did you visit most often?

• Visit house

• Play there

Simple Toys

We treasured simple things – a cherished doll, wooden blocks, metal cars that lasted forever. Imagination made them magical.

What playthings filled your childhood? Tell us about the toys, both store-bought and homemade, that sparked your imagination.

What was your most precious store-bought toy?

- Favorite bought toy

- When you got it

What dolls or stuffed animals kept you company?

- Favorite dolls

- Stuffed animals

Which toy did everyone in the neighborhood want?

- What everyone wanted

- Trendy playthings

Childhood Clothes

Clothes were fewer but made to last - Sunday best kept pristine, play clothes patched and passed down, special outfits that marked occasions. Each item had its purpose and story.

What did little ones wear in those days? Share about everyday outfits, special occasion clothes, and hand-me-downs that were part of life.

What did you wear for everyday activities?

• Play clothes

• Home dress

How did your family handle special occasion outfits?

• Holiday clothes

• Style choices

What shoes did children wear back then?

• Types of shoes

• Taking care of shoes

Family Meals

Meals were more than food – they were gatherings, lessons in manners, sharing of daily stories. We ate what was served and learned the art of family conversation.

What foods graced your childhood table? Tell us about typical meals, special dishes, and the rules children followed at mealtime.

What did breakfast look like in your home?

• Morning breakfast

• What kids ate

Who cooked the daily meals regularly?

• Who cooked meals

• Helping in kitchen

What mealtime rules did children follow?

• Eating manners

• Mealtime behavior

Old-Time Sweets

Treats were special then - penny candy from the corner store, home-made cookies warm from the oven, summer's ice cream truck music that sent us running.

What treats made your eyes light up? Share about the candies, desserts, and special snacks that brightened your early years.

What penny candies could children buy then?

• Sweet shops

• Popular choices

How did your family make homemade desserts?

• Family desserts

• Baking together

What treats marked special occasions?

• Holiday sweets

• Birthday treats

Outdoor Adventures

Our playground was the wide world – climbing trees, building forts, chasing fireflies. Every day brought new discoveries in fields, woods, and backyard kingdoms.

Where did your outdoor play take you? Tell us about the games, explorations, and natural wonders that filled your days outside.

Where did neighborhood children gather daily?

• Where kids gathered

• Favorite spots

What adventures did nearby nature offer?

• Nature spots

• Wild finds

What natural treasures did children collect?

• Pretty rocks

• Cool sticks

Early Dreams

"All our dreams can come true if we have the courage to pursue them." - Walt Disney

What did you imagine becoming? Remember those first dreams and aspirations that filled your young mind.

What job did you first dream of having?

• What you wanted to be

• Why you liked it

Who was your biggest real-life hero?

• Who you looked up to

• Why they inspired

What skills did you eagerly want to learn?

• Skills you wished for

• Things to try

3

School Days & Simple Ways

Hand-sewn lunch bags and pigtail ribbons, best friends sharing secrets and dreams. Those precious school days shaped you with gentle lessons and heartfelt laughter.

First Day at School

That first morning remains clear - new shoes, packed lunch, butter-flies in my stomach. Little did I know how those steps would shape my life.

Take us back to that memorable first day. What emotions do you remember as you stepped into your classroom for the very first time?

Share about packing your school bag the night before.

• School bag packing

• Clothes ready for tomorrow

What did your classroom look like when you first walked in that morning?

• Desks and blackboard

• Teacher's corner

How did students travel to school in your day?

• Transport methods

• Walking routes

The School Building

Our schoolhouse stood proud and solid – red brick walls, tall windows, wooden floors that creaked with stories.

Describe your school as it was then. What details stand out - the halls, the classrooms, the playground, and those special corners where memories were made?

What did your school building look like from the outside?

• Front gates

• Walls and windows

Where did students gather before class and during breaks?

• Meeting spots

• Play areas

What made certain spots in school special to you?

• Favorite places

• Memory corners

Favorite Teachers

"A good teacher can inspire hope, ignite the imagination, and instill a love of learning." - Brad Henry

Which teachers left lasting impressions? Share about the educators whose wisdom, kindness, or unique teaching style made a difference in your life.

What made your favorite teacher's lessons different from others?

• Teaching methods

• Class activities

What creative ways did teachers make difficult lessons interesting?

• Making hard things easy

• Learning games

How did teachers reward good work and encourage students?

• Stars and stickers

• Special helper jobs

Classroom Friends

Friendship bloomed differently in those school days – sharing pencils, passing notes, studying together. Some of those classroom bonds grew into connections that still warm my heart.

Who shared your school days? Tell us about the friendships formed over shared pencils, playground games, and classroom activities.

Who was your first friend at school and how did you meet?

• First meeting

• Friend story

What games did you play with friends during break time?

• Group games

• Break activities

How did you help each other with school work?

• Homework together

• Sharing notes

School Supplies

As summer wanes, backpacks fill with fresh supplies - new pencils, clean notebooks, and textbooks. These simple tools open worlds of learning.

What tools filled your school bag? Remember the books, pencils, and special items that equipped you for learning in those days.

What kind of bag did you carry school items in?

• Bag type

• Pencil case

What basic supplies did every student need for daily lessons?

• Writing tools

• Class materials

How did students organize and protect their textbooks?

• Cover wrapping

• Storage methods

Lunchtime Stories

Lunch breaks were about more than food - trading sandwich halves, sharing stories, playing quick games. These informal moments taught us as much about friendship as any lesson.

How did you spend your lunch breaks? Tell us about the meals, trades, conversations, and games that made this time special.

What foods were common in lunch boxes during your school days?

• Typical meals

• Food choices

Where did students gather to eat their lunch together?

• Lunch room tables

• Outside benches

How did children share or trade lunch items with friends?

• Trading snacks

• Giving treats

Favorite Subjects

Some subjects sang to my soul - whether it was stories in English class or discoveries in science. Learning became joy when passion met purpose.

Which lessons captured your interest? Remember the subjects that sparked your curiosity and joy in learning.

Which subject made you most excited to go to class?

• Favorite subject

• Fun lessons

How did teachers make your favorite subject come alive?

• Interesting projects

• Cool activities

What special projects or assignments do you still remember?

• Special assignments

• Class shows

School Activities

Special programs colored our school days - spelling bees, science fairs, class plays. Each event challenged us to discover talents we didn't know we had.

What special programs enriched your school days? Share about the clubs, sports, or events that added excitement to your education.

What special events brought the whole school together?

• School festivals

• Sports days

Which sports or physical activities did students participate in?

• Team games

• Exercise time

What performances or shows did students prepare for?

• School plays

• Music concerts

After School Fun

When the final bell rang, adventures began - games on the play-ground, walks home with friends, activities that bridged school and home life with joy.

How did you spend your time after the bell rang? Share about the activities, friendships, and adventures that followed school hours.

What was your usual route home from school each day?

• Walking routes

• Friend groups

Where did children gather to play after school ended?

• Friend's yard

• Park games

What homework routines did you follow at home?

• Study time

• Evening lessons

School Celebrations

School events marked our year - holiday programs, field days, end-of-term parties. These celebrations brought our community together, making school more than just lessons.

What special events brightened the school year? Remember the performances, parties, and programs that created lasting memories.

What holiday celebrations did your school organize each year?

• Holiday events

• Special customs

How did students participate in school performances or shows?

• Stage events

• Show preparation

What decorations and preparations made school events memorable?

• Room decorations

• Celebration preparations

Graduation Pride

"Education is the most powerful weapon which you can use to change the world." - Nelson Mandela

What memories stand out from completing school? Share about the ceremonies, celebrations, and feelings that marked this milestone.

What special outfits or items did graduates wear that day?

• Special outfit

• Ceremony clothes

How did families celebrate students' graduation success?

• Party at home

• Proud photos

What gifts or cards did graduates commonly receive?

• Memory books

• Special presents

4

Finding Your Place

With hope in your heart and dreams in your pocket, you stepped into the world. Each challenge made you stronger, each triumph sweeter, as you discovered your-self.

Spreading Wings

Independence came in small steps – staying out later, making my own decisions, feeling the thrill of choosing my path. Every decision a step toward becoming.

When did you first feel truly independent? Tell us about the experiences that made you feel grown-up and ready for life.

Where did you live when you first moved out?

- First apartment/room

- Living by yourself

What new skills did you learn while living alone?

- Cooking methods

- Home maintenance

What daily challenges surprised you most?

- Unexpected problems

- Learning moments

Solo Travels

Every solo adventure brought insights about independence, bravery, and the thrill of exploring unfamiliar territories. These experiences molded both inner strength and perspective.

What paths did you venture down by yourself? Share the destinations you discovered and the self-assurance you developed.

Describe your initial independent journey.

• First steps alone

• Finding your way

Tell us about surprising travel challenges.

• Obstacles encountered

• How you adapted

Tell us about memorable local encounters.

• People you met

• Conversations shared

Time of Your Own

Managing my own schedule brought both freedom and responsibility. Learning to balance work, rest, and play taught me about priorities and the precious nature of time.

How did you organize your days when you began managing your own schedule? Remember learning to balance responsibilities and freedom.

How did you plan your meals during the week?

• Grocery shopping

• Weekly cooking

What activities filled your weekends?

• Weekend hobbies

• Social events

What did you do for recreation after work?

• Evening relaxing

• Fun activities

Money in Hand

Remember your first earnings or allowance? Share how it felt to have your own money and the choices you made with it.

What was your first regular source of income?

- Income source

- Work type

How did you decide what to buy first?

- Purchase choices

- Shopping plans

What special items did you save up for?

- Saving goals

- Dream items

Learning to Save

Understanding the value of money came through small decisions – save or spend, wait or buy, need or want.

How did you first grasp the basics of managing money? Describe your journey between spending choices and saving habits.

When did you hit your first savings target, and what steps led you there?

• Target achieved

• Path to success

How did you manage fun with friends while keeping savings on track?

• Wise spending

• Financial priorities

Tell us about your most significant early money decision.

• Key moment

• Long-term impact

Mirror Moments

"To be yourself in a world that is constantly trying to make you something else is the greatest accomplishment." - Ralph Waldo Emerson

When did you begin developing your own style? Tell us about finding your personal fashion sense and expressing yourself.

What clothing styles were popular in your youth?

• Popular clothes

• Young trends

Where did you shop for your clothes?

• Shopping spots

• Store choices

How did you style your hair back then?

• Style choices

• Care routine

Life Skills

Independence required mastering many skills - from budgeting to basic repairs, time management to decision-making. Each new ability built confidence and capability.

What essential abilities did you develop? Remember learning to handle daily tasks and responsibilities on your own.

What basic repairs did you learn to handle?

• Fix-it skills

• Home maintenance

How did you learn to cook for yourself?

• Cooking basics

• Kitchen skills

What health habits did you develop?

• Self care

• Good habits

Circle of Friends

Who formed your support system? Remember the friendships that helped shape your journey into adulthood.

Where did you meet your closest friends?

• Meeting places

• Friend circles

What activities did you enjoy together?

• Group fun

• Shared hobbies

How did you stay in touch regularly?

• Communication methods

• Meeting times

Young Heart's Dreams

Dreams then were both practical and wild – some achieved, some changed, some let go, but all part of discovering what really mattered to my heart.

What hopes filled your heart then? Share about the dreams and ambitions that inspired your young adult years.

What career path interested you most?

• Dream job

• Career path

How did you plan for your future?

• Future planning

• Life goals

Which role models inspired you then?

• Good example

• Admired people

First Job

Take us through your entry into the professional world. What surprised you, challenged you, or made you proud?

Tell us about your first job interview experience.

• How you prepared

• What happened

What surprised you most about your first workplace?

• New discoveries

• Real work life

What early mistake taught you an important lesson?

• What went wrong

• What you learned

Career Presence

> *Building a career identity meant more than just dressing the part – it was about finding confidence, voice, and presence in the professional world.*

How did you develop your workplace presence? Share about finding your professional voice and style.

Share your turning points in professional growth.

- Challenge faced

- Recognition gained

Share about learning workplace communication.

- Speaking up

- Being heard

What professional image adjustments surprised you?

- New adjustments

- Growth shown

5

When Hearts Were Young

Like a favorite love song, your heart recognized its melody in Grandpa's smile. Together, you danced into a future bright with promise and endless possibilities.

First Crush

Like petals unfurling in spring sunshine, those tender feelings bloomed into more than sweet whispers - they painted the world in new colors of wonder.

How did you handle these new feelings? Share about finding your way through first attractions and young romance.

Tell us about the moments that made your heart stop.

• Unexpected encounters

• Unplanned conversations

Share about learning to express interest.

• Shy hellos

• Quiet signals

What did you learn about yourself during this time?

• Surprising discoveries

• Unexpected growth

Meeting Grandpa

Take us back to when you first met Grandpa. What caught your attention? Share about that initial meeting and the feelings it stirred.

What were you doing when you first met Grandpa?

• Special occasion

• Chance encounter

What was Grandpa wearing that day?

• Clothing style

• First impression

What did you two first talk about?

• Opening words

• Common interests

Special Dates

Dating was different then. Every meeting was precious, planned, and filled with sweet anticipation.

Where did young couples go for dates? Share about the places, activities, and simple pleasures that filled your courtship.

What popular places did young couples visit then?

• Dating spots

• Common hangouts

How did you two spend weekends together?

• Weekend activities

• Regular places

What kind of movies did you watch together?

• Movie genres

• Favorite films

Stay Connected

Through whispered words, shared songs, and gentle signals, we find countless ways to touch each other's hearts - distance merely a challenge to overcome.

How did you stay in touch between meetings? Remember the ways you expressed your growing feelings when apart.

What was your favorite way to stay connected during those days?

- How you connected

- Sweet moments

When could you make phone calls?

- Call times

- Phone conversations

What small gifts did you exchange?

- Gift choices

- Sweet surprises

Bridal Clothes

My wedding dress was dreams woven into reality, traditions honored, new beginnings clothed in white. Every detail held meaning and memory.

What did brides wear in those days? Share about choosing your wedding attire and the styles that were popular then.

How did you choose your wedding dress?

• Dress shopping

• Style selection

What shoes and accessories completed your look?

• Wedding accessories

• Bridal shoes

Who helped you prepare your outfit?

• Family help

• Friend support

The Big Day

Our wedding day dawned with promise – nervous excitement, happy tears, countless details coming together in a celebration of love and commitment.

Paint a picture of your wedding day. Tell us about the ceremony, the special moments, and the emotions that filled your heart.

What time did your wedding day begin?

• Morning prep

• Day schedule

What food was served to guests?

• Wedding menu

• Special dishes

What unexpected things happened?

• Surprise moments

• Special memories

Honeymoon Tales

Those first days as husband and wife were filled with discovery - learning to say "we" instead of "I," creating our own traditions, beginning our story together.

What adventures marked your first days as newlyweds? Share about beginning your life together and creating new memories.

Where did you spend your honeymoon?

• Place name

• Trip length

How did you travel there?

• Transport method

• Journey details

What souvenirs did you bring home?

• Special items

• Memory pieces

First Home Together

Creating our first home meant blending two lives – his chair with my curtains, our shared dreams filling empty rooms with possibility and promise.

How did you create your first shared home? Tell us about setting up housekeeping and blending your lives together.

Where was your first home located?

- Home location

- Neighborhood

What furniture did you start with?

- Basic items

- Essential pieces

How did you decorate your space?

- Home decor

- Style choices

Young Couple Dreams

Together we dreamed bigger than we ever had alone - planning futures, imagining family, building hopes that would guide our journey through the years ahead.

What hopes did you share for your future? Remember the dreams and plans you made together as newlyweds.

How did you picture your family?

• Family plans

• Future children

What savings goals did you set?

• Money plans

• Financial goals

What travel plans excited you?

• Trip wishes

• Holiday dreams

6

Becoming a Mother

First tiny fingerprints on your heart, soft breaths against your shoulder. Motherhood opened a chamber in your soul you never knew existed, filling it with boundless love.

Precious Gifts

"Making the decision to have a child is momentous. It is to decide forever to have your heart go walking around outside your body." - *Elizabeth Stone*

Tell us about each of your children. Share what made each one unique and special from the very beginning.

What special skills or talents did each of your children show early?

• Born talents

• Unique traits

How did each child's personality differ when they were small?

• Character traits

• Personal style

What nicknames did you give each child and why?

• Nicknames

• Name origins

Mother's Touch

What parenting practices did you follow? Tell us about your approach to caring for and nurturing your little ones.

What daily routines helped you manage all your children's needs?

• Time management

• Daily tasks

How did you handle common childhood illnesses and injuries?

• Medical care

• Health practices

How did you make sure each child felt special and loved?

• Quality time

• Love showing

Children's Rooms

Creating spaces for our children was an act of love - choosing colors, arranging furniture, making each room a safe haven for growth and dreams.

How did you arrange space for your growing family? Remember creating special places for your children in your home.

How did you make each child's space feel personal?

- Room themes

- Special items

Where did the children do homework and play?

- Study corner

- Play areas

How did room arrangements change as children grew older?

- Furniture moves

- Room adjustments

Childhood Clothes

Dressing children was both practical and precious - tiny outfits for special days, play clothes meant to survive adventure, hand-me-downs carrying memories from child to child.

What went into dressing your children then? Share about shopping, hand-me-downs, and keeping growing children clothed.

Where did you shop for special occasion outfits?

• Party clothes

• Event outfits

How did you handle rapid growth and changing sizes?

• Clothing plans

• Size changes

What clothing items did you learn to fix or make?

• Repair skills

• DIY clothing

Family Home

Our home evolved with our growing family - spaces adapted, walls witnessed milestones, rooms filled with laughter. It was our anchor in life's storms.

What made your family's living space special? Remember how you created a nurturing environment for your children to grow.

What spaces did you create for family activities together?

• Family spots

• Activity areas

How did you make the kitchen work for family meals?

• Meal space

• Food serving

What safety changes did you make for young children?

• Safety measures

• Lock systems

School Years

"Education is not preparation for life; education is life itself." – John Dewey

How did you support your children's education? Remember helping with homework, attending school events, and encouraging learning.

What morning routine helped get children ready for school?

- Getting ready

- Morning tasks

What school events did you regularly attend?

- School shows

- Parent days

How did you handle school lunch preparation?

- Lunch packing

- Food choices

Proud Moments

Every achievement, big or small, filled my heart. Watching my children grow and flourish brought joy beyond measure.

What achievements brought joy to your heart? Share about the milestones and accomplishments that made you proud as a mother.

What first steps did each child master independently?

• First actions

• New abilities

How did you celebrate your children's school achievements?

• Celebrations

• Award moments

Which sports or activities did your children excel in?

• Best sports

• Top hobbies

7

The Heart of Our Home

Love flowed from your kitchen like warm honey, sweet and nurturing. Your gentle touch made our house a haven, where every meal was seasoned with tenderness.

Family Gatherings

When did your family come together? Share about those special occasions when everyone gathered and the traditions that made them memorable.

What holiday traditions did your family create and follow each year?

• Holiday customs

• Special celebrations

How did you prepare your home for big family gatherings?

• House preparation

• Space arrangement

What games or activities did everyone enjoy together?

• Group activities

• Popular games

Weekend Joys

Weekends were precious times of togetherness - family projects, shared adventures, special treats. These breaks from routine strengthened our bonds.

What made weekends special? Tell us about family activities and traditions that made these days different from the rest.

What regular weekend activities did your family most enjoy?

• Saturday plans

• Regular trips

What special breakfast treats did you make on weekends?

• Special pancakes

• Weekend treats

Where did your family go for weekend entertainment?

• Entertainment spots

• Family venues

Holiday Magic

"Traditions touch us, they connect us, and they expand us." – *Rita Barreto Craig*

How did you celebrate special occasions? Remember the ways you made holidays meaningful and magical for your family.

What decorations transformed your home during different holidays?

• Holiday decor

• Festive touches

How did you organize gift-giving within the family?

• Gift giving rules

• Present customs

What special clothes did everyone wear for holidays?

• Celebration wear

• Dress codes

Kitchen Treasures

Our family recipes were love letters written in ingredients and heritage preserved in careful measurements and handwritten notes.

What recipes became family favorites? Share about the special dishes that brought comfort and joy to your loved ones.

What everyday meals did your family request most often?

- Popular meals

- Most requested

What kitchen tools were most important for family cooking?

- Important utensils

- Key appliances

What recipes did you create or modify yourself?

- Own creations

- Family recipes

Family Table

Our dining table witnessed daily life unfold - morning rushes, evening debriefings, homework sessions, celebration feasts. It was where we shared not just meals, but our lives.

What memories were made around your table? Tell us about mealtime conversations and the warmth of sharing food together.

What mealtime rules helped bring the family together daily?

• Dinner rules

• Table manners

What conversation topics filled your family mealtimes?

• Table talk

• Family sharing

What special items decorated your family dining table?

• Table settings

• Special items

Evening Routines

Nighttime brought its own ceremonies - homework check-ins, story sharing, quiet conversations, bedtime prayers. These gentle endings wove our days together.

How did your family end each day? Share about nighttime rituals and ways you helped everyone wind down together.

What helped your children prepare for bedtime smoothly?

• Night steps

• Sleep prep

How did your family spend time together before bed?

• Family reading

• Evening talks

What bedtime stories or songs became family favorites?

• Favorite books

• Bedtime songs

Seasonal Customs

Each season brought its own traditions - spring cleaning, summer picnics, autumn harvests, winter celebrations. Nature's rhythm guided our family calendar.

How did your family mark the changing seasons? Share about traditions and activities that celebrated each time of year.

What spring activities marked the start of warmer days?

• Spring traditions

• Garden work

How did your family enjoy summer's long, warm days?

• Summer fun

• Vacation activities

What fall traditions did your family create together?

• Fall activities

• Harvest fun

How did you prepare your home for winter months?

• Winter prep

• Cold weather plans

8

Life's Second Blooming

Each grandchild's smile brings sunrise to your world anew. Their little arms around your neck remind you that love multiplies with every generation's embrace.

Special Qualities

Each of you shines with unique light. Let me tell you what I see in each of you, the beauty that makes you uniquely precious.

What makes each grandchild uniquely wonderful? Remember the distinct traits and gifts you see in each one.

What special talent or interest does each grandchild show strongly?

• Unique skills

• Personal interests

What activities do you enjoy most with each grandchild?

• Shared activities

• Fun together

What nickname have you given to each grandchild?

• Special calls

• Name meanings

Story Times

"Stories are a way to preserve one's self. To be remembered. And to forget." - Sandra Cisneros

What stories do you share with your grandchildren? Tell us about the special moments of storytelling and passing down family tales.

What childhood stories do your grandchildren ask to hear?

- Requested stories

- Memory tales

What special spot do you use for storytelling?

- Reading place

- Story spots

Which family history stories fascinate your grandchildren most?

- Past events

- Family history

Sweet Treats

Special snacks became our secret language of love – cookies warm from the oven, favorite fruits cut just so, little surprises that said "grandmother loves you" without words.

What special snacks do you prepare for your grandchildren? Share about the treats and traditions that make visits to grandma's special.

What quick snacks do you always have ready?

· Ready foods

· Quick treats

How do grandchildren help you make special treats?

· Helper tasks

· Cooking fun

What recipes have become grandchildren's favorites?

· Liked sweets

· Often asked

Secret Recipes

These family recipes carry more than ingredients - they hold stories, memories, traditions. May they bring comfort and connection to future generations.

How do you pass down family food traditions? Remember teaching your grandchildren special recipes and kitchen wisdom.

What family recipes do you want grandchildren to learn?

• Must-learn dishes

• Family meals

What cooking shortcuts have you discovered to share?

• Helpful hints

• Quick methods

Which recipes bring back your own childhood memories?

• Memory meals

• Past favorites

Teaching Moments

Wisdom flows naturally when hearts are open - life lessons wrapped in gentle words, values taught through everyday moments, love showing the way.

What life lessons do you share? Tell us about the gentle ways you guide and teach your grandchildren.

What simple skills do you teach during everyday activities?

• Basic tasks

• Life learning

What traditional crafts or hobbies do you teach?

• Craft teaching

• Skill sharing

How do you encourage good manners and kindness?

• Good habits

• Value lessons

Play Days

Playing with grandchildren brought magic back to ordinary moments - seeing wonder through their eyes, finding joy in simple things, creating memories in shared laughter.

What activities do you enjoy with your grandchildren? Share about the games, crafts, and fun that fill your time together.

What outdoor games do your grandchildren love playing together?

• Garden games

• Lawn fun

What indoor games work best on rainy days?

• Home games

• Inside fun

What seasonal activities do grandchildren especially enjoy?

• Summer play

• Winter fun

Treasure Box

Keeping special items for grandchildren - toys, books, little surprises - became a way of holding memories and creating moments of joy.

What special items do you keep for grandchildren visits? Tell us about the toys, books, and treasures that make your home special to them.

What toys stay permanently at grandma's house and why?

• House toys

• Play keepers

Which books have become favorites for reading together?

• Loved books

• Reading picks

How do you store special artwork or crafts?

• Art saving

• Craft keeping

9

Pastimes & Precious Moments

In quiet afternoons and gentle pursuits, you found joy in creating beauty. Every stitch, every flower planted, every recipe perfected was another way to share your love.

Creative Hands

"Creativity is intelligence having fun." - *Albert Einstein*

What crafts and creations bring you joy? Share about the handmade projects that have filled your leisure time.

What kind of sewing or needlework projects did you enjoy making at home?

• Sewing projects

• Craft types

How did you learn your first craft skill and who taught you?

• First crafts

• Who taught

Which handmade gifts have you created for special family occasions?

• Made gifts

• Special makes

Garden Pleasures

"A garden is a grand teacher. It teaches patience and careful watch-fulness." - Gertrude Jekyll

How has gardening enriched your life? Tell us about your experiences with plants, flowers, and growing things.

What was your first garden like, and where did you start it?

• First plants

• Start location

Which vegetables or flowers have been easiest for you to grow?

• Best plants

• Easy growing

What garden tools have become your most trusted helpers outdoors?

• Used tools

• Must-haves

Kitchen Projects

What special dishes do you enjoy making? Remember your favorite recipes and cooking adventures beyond daily meals.

What was the first special recipe you learned to cook perfectly?

• First dish

• Best cooking

How did you organize your recipe collection and save family favorites?

• Recipe files

• Family collections

What cooking disasters turned into funny family stories later?

• Kitchen mishaps

• Funny failures

Friends & Coffee

Coffee gatherings were about connection, shared stories, laughter, and support. These moments with friends seasoned life with joy.

How do you enjoy time with friends? Share about social gatherings, coffee dates, and maintaining friendships.

Where did you usually meet friends for regular get-togethers and chats?

• Meeting spots

• Regular places

What special treats did you serve when friends visited your home?

• Served food

• Guest snacks

Which friend group activities became regular traditions over years?

• Group plans

• Friend traditions

Movie Memories

"Movies are like an expensive form of therapy for me." - Tim Burton

What kinds of films capture your interest? Tell us about your favorite movies and how entertainment has changed over time.

Which movies have remained your favorites throughout your life?

- Best films

- Life favorites

What was different about going to movies when you were young?

- Old theaters

- Past shows

How did you usually spend movie nights with family or friends?

- Watch parties

- Movie nights

Music & Songs

Certain songs became the soundtrack of my life - hymns that lifted spirits, dance tunes that brought joy, lullabies passed through generations.

What music moves your heart? Remember the songs, artists, and musical moments that have meant the most to you.

What songs always remind you of special moments in life?

• Life songs

• Special tunes

Which musical instruments did you or family members play?

• Music skills

• Family players

Where did you usually go to hear live music performances?

• Show places

• Concert spots

Reading Corner

"Reading gives us someplace to go when we have to stay where we are." - Mason Cooley

What role have books played in your life? Share about your reading interests and memorable stories that touched you.

What types of books became your go-to choices?

• Loved genres

• Regular reads

Which magazines or newspapers did your family regularly read?

• News choices

• Regular papers

Where was your special place for quiet reading at home?

• Reading place

• Quiet spot

Travel Tales

Each journey, near or far, added colors to my life canvas - new sights, different cultures, unexpected discoveries that broadened my world.

What places have you explored? Remember the journeys and destinations that have broadened your horizons.

What was your first big trip away from your hometown?

- First trip

- Early visits

Which mode of transportation was your favorite for family trips?

- Travel type

- Going ways

What unexpected adventures happened during your memorable travels?

- Travel surprises

- Journey stories

Collection Stories

My collections tell stories of life's journey – precious items gathered over years, each piece holding memories and meaning beyond its simple form.

What items have you collected over time? Share about the special things you've gathered and why they matter to you.

How did you display or store your special collections at home?

• Show setup

• Keep safe

Which items in your collection have interesting stories behind them?

• Item stories

• Memory pieces

Where did you usually find new pieces for your collections?

• Shop spots

• Find places

Exercise Ways

Staying active became a celebration of life – morning walks, gentle exercises, dance movements that kept body and spirit young.

How do you stay active and healthy? Tell us about your approach to physical activity and maintaining wellness.

Which daily tasks naturally kept you physically active?

• Daily movement

• Active chores

What simple exercises have worked best for you over time?

• Favorite moves

• Regular routines

Where did you usually go for walks or outdoor activities?

• Walk routes

• Outside spots

Learning New

What new skills have you developed? Share about learning experiences and expanding your abilities over time.

What new skill or hobby surprised you by becoming a favorite?

• Found hobby

• Surprise skills

How did you find time to learn new things while raising family?

• Study time

• Learn when

Which modern technologies have you learned to use successfully?

• Tech learning

• New devices

10

From My Heart to Yours

Like precious family recipes, these gathered wisdoms are seasoned with love and time. I share them tenderly, hoping they'll nourish your heart as they've nourished mine.

Family Values

"Values are like fingerprints. Nobody's are the same, but you leave them all over everything you do." - Elvis Presley

What principles matter most to pass forward? Remember the core values you hope will guide their life choices.

What simple rules have helped guide your daily life decisions?

- Life principles

- Daily wisdom

What practical habits would you recommend for a happy life?

- Good habits

- Life practices

What work attitudes helped you succeed in different situations?

- Work ethics

- Success habits

Life Lessons

Life has taught me precious truths - about love's power, courage's importance, joy's simplicity. These lessons are my gift to you, learned through living.

What key wisdom would you share? Write about the most important life lessons you want them to understand.

What early mistakes taught you the most valuable lessons?

• Best lessons

• Growth moments

How did you handle big changes and challenges successfully?

• Change handling

• Problem solving

What simple truths have proven most reliable over time?

• Basic wisdom

• Proven truths

Time's Value

> *Time taught its own lessons - about priorities, presence, the price of rushing, and the value of moments fully lived.*

How has your view of time evolved? Remember the realizations about what truly matters and deserves our time.

What activities have proven most worthwhile spending time on?

• Best uses

• Worth doing

How did you balance family time with other responsibilities?

• Life balance

• Time splits

Which moments do you wish you had spent more time on?

• Missed chances

• Time regrets

Faith Journey

"Faith is taking the first step even when you don't see the whole staircase." - Martin Luther King Jr.

How has your spiritual understanding grown? Tell us about the development of your faith and beliefs over time.

How did your faith help during difficult life moments?

• Tough times

• Faith support

What spiritual practices became important parts of your routine?

• Daily rituals

• Prayer times

How has your understanding of faith changed over years?

• Faith growth

• Belief changes

Joy Sources

What have you learned about finding happiness? Share your insights about creating and maintaining joy in life.

What simple pleasures have brought you consistent daily happiness?

• Daily joys

• Simple pleasures

How did you maintain cheerfulness during challenging situations?

• Tough times

• Stay happy

Where did you usually go to lift your spirits?

• Happy spots

• Mood lifts

Heart Wishes

My dreams for you are like stars - countless, bright, and full of possibility. Not for specific paths, but for lives filled with purpose, love, and joy.

What dreams do you hold for their futures? Tell them about your deepest hopes and wishes for their lives ahead.

What basic life skills would you want them to master?

• Life skills

• Must-know

How do you hope they'll handle life's tough challenges?

• Problem solving

• Challenge facing

Which character traits would you most want them to grow?

• Good traits

• Strong heart

Grandpa's Edition Available

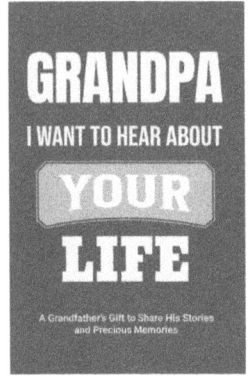

Grandpa, I Want to Hear About Your Life

Ever wonder about the young boy who became your wise grandfather? The courage of his early adventures? The moment his heart knew Grandma was the one? This heartwarming companion to our Grandma edition reveals another treasured chapter of your family's legacy.

Through thoughtfully crafted chapters, discover the quiet strength and enduring wisdom of your grandfather's journey. Every page captures the essence of a life built with determination and guided by love.

Our "Family Story" collection also includes the beloved **Mom and Dad editions.**

Don't let these treasured tales slip away. Give a gift that will inspire generations to come. Because every grandfather's story is a legacy of wisdom worth preserving.

Available at major online bookstores:

- Amazon

- Barnes & Noble

- and other leading online retailers